Mind Over

The Psychology of Athletic Success

Head Chatter

A Six Week Course

by
Greg Justice, MA

MIND OVER HEAD CHATTER: A SIX-WEEK COURSE TO ATHLETIC SUCCESS

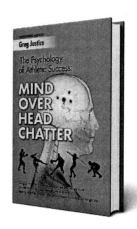

OVERVIEW

Ever thought that being a successful athlete boiled down to nothing more than talent?

Have you found yourself buckling under the pressure of being an athlete and giving in to the self-doubt and anxiety that may be clouding your mind?

That's precisely why you should be glad you picked up this *Mind Over Head Chatter* companion course!

UPON COMPLETION OF THIS SIX-WEEK COURSE, YOU'LL KNOW HOW TO:

1. Ignite your passion so you can go after your goals.

2. Achieve a winning mindset – the kind that can help you become mentally tough when you need it the most.

3. Have the kind of support group that will help you remain confident and motivated, no matter the circumstances.

4. Set the most powerful goals on your journey to athletic success.

5. Create a personal highlight reel of your achievements, accomplishments and wins in life.

6. Emulate the greatest athletes, from their mental toughness to their discipline and determination.

IN THIS COURSE, WE WILL COVER THE FOLLOWING TOPICS:

- Week One: Building Your Passion

- Week Two: Building Your Social Support

- Week Three: Creating Your Personal Highlight Reel

- Week Four: How To Set Powerful Goals

- Week Five: Building Your Mental Toughness

- Week Six: How to Emulate Great Athletes

INTRODUCTION

As an athlete, you are often asked to handle significant pressure. Pressure to be bigger. Faster. Stronger. With so much pressure weighing in, it's no wonder so many athletes often lose touch with the passion and fire that inspired them to be athletes in the first place.

Athletes may seem outwardly confident in their own skills, but as an athlete yourself, you know that there's plenty of room in your head for self-doubt and anxiety. Perhaps you beat yourself up too much after a race, or maybe you were injured during training and now you're having a hard time getting back into the swing of things. No matter the reason, it's completely normal to find yourself plagued by self-doubt, anxiety, and the pressure to succeed.

Luckily, that's where this six-week course comes into play. This course – designed as a companion piece to *Mind Over Head Chatter* by Greg Justice (that's me!) – is designed to help athletes of all ages, skill sets and talent levels to overcome the prevalent fear and anxiety that can prevent them from achieving real success. Throughout the next six weeks, you will learn the following vital tips and techniques:

- How to get back in touch with the passion that inspired you to become an athlete in the first place.
- How to build a powerful support system that will give you the assistance you need to push harder and faster.
- How to create a personal highlight reel of all your past successes, so you never give in to any of the self-doubt that plagues your head.
- How to set goals that are so powerful, you'll not only achieve them – you'll feel like you were forced to achieve them.
- How to build your mental toughness so that you're able to achieve a "winning mindset" – the kind of mindset that makes it possible for you to push forward in your athletic endeavors while silencing any doubt in your head.
- How to emulate your favorite athlete and learn valuable lessons that can be applied to your own life.

Remember, this six-week course is designed to be a companion piece to *Mind Over Head Chatter*. If you're ever confused about any topics brought up during this course, please refer back to the book to help understand these ideas again. All techniques, tips and ideas in this course are based off the information in my book.

Ready to get started? Then let's move right on to Week One!

WEEK ONE: BUILDING YOUR PASSION

When it comes to achieving greatness, many athletes credit their success to two factors:

1. Having the support of someone important in their lives; and/or

2. Having the kind of passion and motivation that keeps driving them forward.

Whether you're just beginning your journey as an athlete or you already have a few ribbons and medals under your belt, it's important to begin this course by connecting with your passions and identifying your support system. These factors are the things that will give you the fuel to keep fighting, even when the going gets tough.

For example, let's say you're working on shaving 30 minutes from your marathon time. Your next race is in two months – that means you're determined to spend the next eight weeks working on getting faster and stronger. You go for longer runs, you start lifting weights, and you eat as clean a diet as possible in order to give yourself the fuel you need to succeed.

However, when the day of the marathon comes around, you only end up shaving roughly 15 minutes from your time.

So what happens next? Do you just give up and accept that you're always going to be stuck at this level? Or do you touch base with your passions, get support and advice from coaches, family, and loved ones, and keep on with your journey?

By the end of this six-week course, you'll be doing the latter!

Let's start off your first week by identifying one of the best ways to get in touch with the passion and motivation that inspired you to become an athlete in the first place – feeling good about yourself.

It seems like such a simple thing, doesn't it? But it's true; as an athlete, you must feel inherently good about yourself and the things you can accomplish in order to succeed. You need to be your biggest fan. Otherwise, you'll find it all too easy to give into the self-doubt that might still exist in the depths of your mind.

If you feel good about yourself, you're more likely to propel yourself towards your goals, no matter how lofty they seem. There is no crippling self-doubt, there is no negative voice telling you that you can't. Even if those things do creep up every once in awhile, your positive feelings and emotions are more than enough to silence the negative thoughts before they take root.

Now look at the other side of the scale. If you're in a state where you perpetually feel bad about yourself, it's doubtful you'll even set goals due to your belief that you will never attain them.

When you feel bad about yourself, you won't have the strength to stay disciplined when temptation eventually rears its ugly head. For example, you're training for an important meet. Feeling bad about yourself may prevent you from standing strong against eating junk food, staying out late, missing workouts, or not giving your best, each and every workout.

Let's say that you're a basketball coach. You see the following two kinds of athletes:

1. The athletes who will work to the brink of exhaustion. They know that if they push themselves just a bit further, they'll be better rebounders or faster forwards. The hard work, pain and exertion are well worth it, because at the end of the day, they have the kind of self-worth and confidence that gets them through even the most painful practices.

2. The athletes who need an extra push. Now, as a coach, you might not encounter these athletes too often – especially once you get to the collegiate level. By that time, the majority of athletes still competing typically have a strong sense of inner worth. But occasionally, you might come across a student-athlete who struggles with self-esteem issues. It doesn't just affect the athlete – it affects the entire team.

Which athlete do you want to be? Do you want to be the athlete who goes the extra mile to become better in every way? Do you want to end every practice with sweat pouring out of your body and tears in your eyes from pushing yourself to the limit?

Or do you want to be the athlete who needs to be pushed by a coach to succeed? The one who might cost the team a big win, or even the championship?

That's why *Mind Over Head Chatter* is designed to help you turn off the self-doubt and transform your brain into one of the biggest assets you'll use to achieve athletic success!

Let's start by analyzing how to build up your self-confidence so you can get back in touch with your passion and what motivated you in the first place.

When you don't feel good about yourself or believe that you're not worthy of your accomplishments, it sends a signal to the world that you shouldn't be treated with respect and love. It tells the world that you can be taken advantage of because you won't stand up for yourself. It shows everybody that you're not truly ready to unlock your athletic potential.

...Because deep down, you believe you don't deserve to be the best.

But I'm here to tell you otherwise.

It's time to stop letting fear and self-doubt impede your life agenda. It's time to put an end to the tortured doubt and "what-ifs" that circulate your mind every day. You only have this one life to enjoy – there are no timeouts or do-overs. We have one shot to get it right. Isn't that blessing alone enough to make you want to shed the shackles of fear that keep you chained to anything less than your best performance?

Now that I've got you fired up, it's time to identify why you might feel self-doubt and negativity. So what is the number one cause of why you're suffering from this self-doubt rather than enjoying a truly stellar athletic performance?

It's simple: you've disconnected from your life.

When you're truly engaged in your life – that means taking advantage of the numerous blessings, friendships, and opportunities that are presented to you each and every day – there's just no time for negativity; you naturally feel good. That's partially why experts recommend keeping busy after a devastating break-up or loss – our body's natural response to keeping busy is to be positive.

But that kind of engagement is superficial at best. The life engagement I'm talking about here means being 110% involved with your game and appreciating everything that's been thrown your way – be it for better or for worse.

If you're disengaged from your life, it may feel disingenuous or pointless to shift back into gear. Yet with time, effort and a little introspection, you'll find yourself truly connecting with the beautiful world around you and all of its many wonders and blessings. As a result, you'll start to feel good about yourself again.

This can have a trickle-down effect on your athletic performance. When you feel good about who you are as a person, you feel better about who you are as an athlete. There's no separation between the two. Your personal life has a direct impact on your athletic life, and vice versa.

Exercise 1.1

Don't believe that your athletic performance is suffering from inner anxieties and doubts? Let's take a closer look. This exercise will help identify the non-productive mind chatter that might be holding you back from achieving athletic success. Answer the following questions:

When you woke up this morning, were you excited to start your day? If not, what made you avoid the tasks ahead? Anxieties? Fears?

_____

_____

_____

Do you feel like you have everything you need to succeed? If not, what is lacking?

_____

_____

_____

Have you ever felt like giving up your sport after a bad practice or performance? Explain why.

_____

_____

_____

What drives you to excel? Does it come from deep inside you or from outside expectations or pressures or people? Describe it.

_____

_____

_____

Do you have any memories from your past that seem to stay with you and adversely affect your life now? List them below…

_____

_____

_____

What does your athletic passion feel like? Would you participate in your sport even if you had no one cheering you on?

_____

_____

Have you ever talked yourself out of trying something new? Of setting a big goal? If so, why?

_____

_____

Any additional thoughts:

_____

_____

Examine your answers to these questions. You'll start to realize that much of what burdens you or bothers you comes from an inward place. In other words, innate fears, doubts and anxieties you have about yourself. That's the root cause of your negativity. Like a weed, we're going to pull this negativity up from the ground and plant a seed of growth, passion, and power in its place.

Take A Closer Look

Let's take a closer look at the feelings that are truly keeping you chained to negativity and how you can release yourself and embrace your inner potential and passion:

Lack Of Focus: Think about the last time you truly wanted something. Didn't the sense of focus make you feel energized? Didn't it give you the motivation you needed to surmount the impossible obstacles that were placed in your path?

Even the greatest athletes can suffer from a lack of focus. But if you want to reignite the passion for your game, you have to get focused on your goals again (don't worry, we'll discuss goal-setting in a later week). Focus will help keep you disciplined and determined, no matter what obstacles might be in your way.

Negative Dialogue: Everyone – and I mean <u>everyone</u> – suffers from negative self-talk at some point in their lives. You know what I'm talking about, the kind of inner dialogue that fills you with doubt, fear and anxiety. However, there's a difference between suffering from and working through an occasional bout of negative dialogue and self-doubt...

...vs. being so crippled by it that it has paralyzed you from achieving your maximum potential.

Negative self-talk can range from a minor annoyance to downright toxic. I'll show you a few examples so you can see just how damaging negative internal dialogue can be:

> "I'll never make varsity. I don't know why I even bother trying."

> "Why don't I ever get first place? Every time I get close, someone else wins. I'll always be in second place."

> "My competitor seems much more accomplished than I am. I might as well give up and save myself the embarrassment."

> "Why should I bother training? I'll never be as good as I want to be."

> "I'll go ahead and let another player on my team take the lead during games. I don't think I'm capable of doing it myself."

> "I lost again. I'm a total loser."

See how this negative self-talk can range from mildly pervasive to toxic and harmful?

No matter what kind of negative inner dialogue you're grappling with, it is highly likely that it is crippling your game. If you want to put an end to the negativity and start feeling better about yourself – and unlock your athletic potential – you have to actively and consciously put an end to the damaging internal dialogue.

You've got to eliminate the negative "mind chatter" and replace it with what I like to call "Elite Talk."

These are the powerful and positive statements you use to replace the negative talk that may be clouding your mind. Here are a few examples of positive inner statements you can make every time your mind starts to go negative on you:

"Bring it on!"

"As long as I stay relaxed and focused, I can master this game."

"Just get the ball to me and I'm going to make good things happen."

"Nothing is going to stand between me and the finish line."

"I hope someone is filming me during this game, because I could be hosting a clinic right now!"

"I know my competition wants me to mess up, but they're going to end up extremely disappointed!"

"I lost this time. Now, what can I do to improve myself and my training so I will win next time?"

This talk is essential for creating the kind of positive internal dialogue that makes the difference between average athletes and great athletes. You need the mindset of a champion, and that can only happen when you fill your brain with positive, uplifting, and inspiring self-talk.

Control Your Mind With Your Body: At first glance, this might sound like an odd technique to use to block out the mental chatter in your mind. But think about how you act right before a big game or a race. Chances are you're completely focused on the task ahead of you. You're staring at the field and imagining yourself succeeding. You've probably stopped talking to others so you can focus on psyching yourself up. You're jumping up and down, warming up your body. Then, right before the game starts – in the last remaining seconds – you tense up, as your whole body is prepared to fight.

In those last few moments, you don't have time to listen to any negative mental chatter that might take up valuable head space. All you can focus on is what's in front of you and how you're going to achieve your best performance ever.

That's exactly what you need to do every time you think negative mental chatter is bringing you down. Your body can help trick your mind into believing that you're more powerful and confident simply because your mind takes cues from your body, and vice versa.

Exercise 1.2

As you read this, slump your shoulders so you're slouching, and frown at this page. Hold that position for a few minutes. Notice what is happening to your emotions.

What does it feel like? Do you feel more tired? Grouchy? Describe it.

_____

_____

Now, sit up straight and put a smile on your face. Hold that position for a few minutes and think about how you feel. Chances are you feel much better. Even if you didn't feel like smiling, it improved your mood didn't it? Did you feel more energy being created?

Our bodies can have a profound impact on our mind's ability to reflect positive or negative thoughts. If your body is aligned with positive and confident body language (straight back, an open and assertive stance, relaxed smile, etc.), it won't take long for your brain to follow suit. When you start to experience negative or annoying mental chatter, use your body to change it. Try shifting your body. Uncross your arms, stand or sit tall, even raise your arms over your head and see how it feels. It might seem a bit unnatural at first, but you'll be surprised how quickly your mental chatter will become silent in the face of your calm and confident pose.

Let's move forward to Week Two. You're about to learn why a personal support system is one of the most powerful tools an athlete can ever have.

Week Two: Building Your Support System

Now that we've identified the best ways to quell any negative mind chatter that might be holding you back, it's time to identify the social support you'll need to remain successful, even when things start getting tough.

This week you'll discover why your relationships matter to your athletic success. Having a strong social network can help fill your mind with the positive self-talk and confidence you need to drive forward. No matter what you want to achieve, you need supportive people on your side.

Exercise 2

Identify the people in your life who offer you encouragement and support. It doesn't have to be an immediate family member; perhaps one of your best friends is always at your games cheering you on. Do you know someone who always listens and doesn't judge you?

Write down the names of at least three to five people who you can count on to be there for you whenever you need them. Then **identify three reasons why you consider these people so supportive.** Be specific. Maybe your mom always greets you at the finish line with a big hug and a sports drink, or perhaps your coach was your rock during a particularly hard time in your personal life.

My Support System:

1. _____

Why?_____

_____

2. _____

Why?_____

_____

3. _____

Why?_____

_____

4. _____

Why?_____

_____

5. _____

Why?_____

_____

6. _____

Why?_____

_____

Keep this list handy – these are the people who are going to help you through your athletic journey – and probably beyond. These people will be there for you no matter what happens. If you ever feel down about yourself, just remember that you have a strong safety net ready to catch you when you fall and give you a push back in the right direction.

It might seem obvious that having a strong social support network will help an athlete build a sense of self-confidence or stick to a rigorous training program. Now, there's research to support the fact that the more people in an athlete's corner, the more likely it is for that athlete to improve his or her success in the game.

Researcher Tim Rees conducted a study to examine how the impact of having a strong social support system helped 200 elite golfers improve their performance. The study found that during anxious and stressful matches, golfers who considered themselves to have strong social support played better than those who did not. The results were certainly apparent – the players lacking social averaged an end-of-round score up to three strokes higher than their counterparts.[1]

These findings suggest that athletes should invest a considerable amount of time in building their social support, as this can have significant pay-offs in the game. So how exactly can you do that?

---

[1] http://sportsmedicine.about.com/od/sportspsychology/qt/Support-Confidence.htm

Here are some techniques to build your support system:

- Ask people to be part of your support group. This might seem obvious, but you'd be surprised at how many family members and friends might not know that you're counting on them. Start with the people you identified in the previous exercise. Identify your goals and plans, then share this information with the people on your list. Once you share your goals, ask them to support you in your endeavors. You may need to define what you mean by support; for example, do you mean having them in the stands when you compete? Driving you to practice? Giving you advice after a bad day? The more specific you are, the more likely it is that you'll receive the kind of support you need down the line.

- Hire a coach. A coach is someone who will push you further than you may be able to push yourself. A coach is the one person who is 100% invested in your success, as his or her own success is reflected in your performance. If you need someone who is always going to be there for you – rain or shine – and understands the intricacies of your sport, then prioritize finding a qualified coach with a track record of success.

- Find a training partner. If you are not able to afford a coach, or you already have one, opt to use a training partner. This person could be someone you've trained with before, or a competitor you're friendly with off the field. Having a training partner can take your game to the next level, since you'll likely compete with him or her during practice. A training partner can push you past your boundaries, which is what you need to improve your athletic performance. What's more, a training partner can help you overcome any mind chatter that might be filling you with self-doubt.

When looking for a training partner, make sure you find someone who competes at a similar level to you. If you really want to challenge yourself, find someone who's slightly better than you. This can give you the push you need during practice to improve your performance, as you'll want to keep up with their level.

- Join a local sports club or organization to meet like-minded people and athletes. This is a great option for someone who may not be competing at the collegiate or professional level, and needs to find new training partners. Socializing with a group who shares a passion for your sport can help broaden your support network, as you could potentially meet training partners, coaches, and people who are happy to cheer you on in the stands.

- Be sure to return the favor. You must be supportive of others in order to build up your own support system. Go to games to cheer them on. Talk to another athlete who just had a bad game or practice. Give them honest encouragement. Think about what you would want to hear. Join with other athletes you know and see if you can form a "support" group of sorts. When you support other athletes, you're much more likely to find people cheering for you.

If you're having trouble building up your support network, analyze your behaviors. You might be driving people away. Should you be the first one to complain during practice or you're always saying something negative about your performance, people might not want to be in your support network simply because they don't want to deal with your negative attitude. This is why it's so important to eliminate negative mind chatter from your brain, as it has likely found its way out of your mouth. If you want to build a strong social support system, you need to be the kind of athlete that people want to support. That means being positive, gracious, and willing to move on, even after a bad game or match.

Now that you've identified the beginnings of your social support network and eliminated some of the negative mind chatter in your head, it's time to move forward with.

The lessons in Week 3 are going to set the foundation for your success. Be sure to incorporate them into your daily life. You'll find that as you grow and improve your athletic performance, your mind chatter will be replaced by positive reinforcement and a strong social support system.

Week Three: Visualize Success
Your Personal Highlight Reel

Now that you've started building your support system, it's time to create your very own personal highlight reel. Think of this as an internal movie that you'll show yourself every time an iota of doubt or nervousness starts to creep into your mind. Your personal highlight reel will be used to remind you of your many successes, and also of your ability to succeed even when that gold medal or blue ribbon seems just out of reach.

I don't care how many trophies you've won or whether you just started training an hour ago. Everyone is capable of making a personal highlight reel. As a human being, you have shown dogged determination in the face of <u>something</u>. It doesn't have to be related to a sport – heck, it doesn't even have to be related to anything athletic at all.

If you've done something to defy the odds...if you've achieved a goal that once seemed far too out of reach...if you've ever done something when other people have told you that you couldn't do it...then you have plenty of material for your personal highlight reel. This week, we're going to focus on building that personal highlight reel, so you will be able to visualize success and remind yourself that you're so much stronger than any obstacles or challenges that may be in your way

You've already achieved wonderful things in your life - things that deserve to be celebrated right here, right now.

How do I know you've done great things? Because I know that right now, you can write down three times in your life that you achieved or overcame something that you thought yourself incapable of.

They don't have to be lofty achievements. In fact, your proudest achievements may have little to do with winning weight-lifting competitions or helping your basketball team earn a conference title. Rather, your greatest achievements could be smaller choices that placed you on the path towards the life that you're leading today.

Exercise 3

Create Your Personal Highlight Reel

It's time to create your list of the accomplishments, small steps, and positive life choices that have helped you become who you are today and the athlete you'll become tomorrow.

Start building your list of accomplishments. To help you get started, here are some examples:

1. "I rose above the taunting of bullies. To them, I appeared weak and vulnerable – but to myself, I knew that I was capable of being so much more than what they said."

2. "I decided to try out for my high school football team, despite all the teasing I endured as a child. They told me I couldn't do it – but as soon as I showed up on that football field, I proved them wrong."

3. "I applied for college. As a first-generation student from a bad part of the city, going to college was pretty much considered a luxury. But I knew I wanted better things for myself – and I didn't stop pushing myself even after I had that acceptance letter in my hands."

See how varied your achievements list can be? It isn't always about earning an award. It's about doing something that helps you rise above the challenges and obstacles in your life. It's about keeping your journey moving forward rather than giving up. It's an accomplishment that should be celebrated – and it's going to form the basis of your highlight reel.

Now it's time to create your own personal highlight reel.

List three to four achievements that you're proud of.
Include both the What and Why. Be specific.

1. _____

_____

_____

2. _____

_____

_____

3. _____

_____

_____

4. _____

_____

_____

Once you've prepared your list, carry it with you or post it where you can see it throughout your day-to-day routine. The more you look at this list, the easier it will be to create that personal highlight reel that you can turn to whenever you need a little extra motivation. It's instantly available in your head – all you have to do is mentally press play to remind yourself of all the amazing successes you've already had in your life.

Your personal highlight reel will help you build momentum towards your goals and help to silence any negative thoughts. It will serve as evidence that you are capable of achieving anything – even if it seems impossible at first.

No matter what is bringing you down, use your personal highlight reel to pick you back up. As you become more and more successful and continue to improve your athletic performance, you can add even more scenes to your reel.

Now let's talk about something that every athlete must have in order to be successful…

Self-Discipline

You can be a "natural" or "gifted" athlete, but if you don't have this one skill, you're eventually going to hit roadblock after roadblock and get stuck while other athletes keep passing you by.

Self-discipline is self-control. Self-discipline allows you to control what is under your control. Discipline isn't the most exciting concept in the so-called "self-help" genre – but it is undeniably the most powerful.

Every athlete will have days when they just don't feel like going to practice, or doing the last 10 reps. When your motivation is lacking, that's when discipline must kick in. Self-discipline allows you to choose reason over desire. Would it be easier to only run 9 laps? Of course! But is it really in your best interest in the long run? The answer is always no.

Without self-discipline, it's easy to get lost on the road towards your ultimate success. Remember, durability is more important than ability.

So what exactly does self-discipline mean?

- For the athlete, self-discipline means doing the work no matter how tired. It means never settling for what's comfortable. Our bodies only change when we push ourselves past our "comfort zone."

- For the single mother, self-discipline means getting up at 4am, no matter how tired she is, to study for her degree before getting her children ready for school.

- For the freelancer, self-discipline means sticking to a work schedule, no matter how tempting it may be to skip work and go to the beach.

- For the weight-loss pursuer, self-discipline means keeping a food journal, eating whole foods and making a commitment to exercise every day - even when stressed or busy.

While these four different people may have separate life goals, they all have one thing in common – they understand that discipline is the key to reaching their goals.

Self-discipline creates consistency. When you practice self-discipline you can stay on track despite distractions. And when you stay on track, you move towards your ultimate goals, no matter what they may be. If success had to be displayed as a formula, it would look a little something like this:

Success = Discipline + A Winning Mindset

As you can see, improving your performance or becoming a successful athlete isn't just about being born with natural talent. It's not about being "lucky" or blessed by a higher power. It has nothing to do with your background, the amount of money you have, or the university you attended.

Instead, it has everything to do with your ability to <u>choose</u> to take action towards your goals each and every day, no matter how small those actions might be. That is what is at the heart of self-discipline – your willingness to choose to better yourself with each passing day.

Success or Failure – It's Your Choice

Now it's time to move on to Week Four. Over the course of the next week, you'll learn how to set powerful goals to motivate yourself during each and every practice. The more goals you set and achieve, the more likely it is that cheers will replace any self-doubt and negative mind chatter!

Week Four: Set Powerful Goals

No athlete becomes successful out of sheer luck; you must create stepping stones to carry you along your pre-determined path. You may have determination and work hard but you need to know where you are going and how you'll get there.

Exercise 4

For many athletes, setting goals doesn't seem like much of a challenge. I'm sure you have at least a general idea of what you'd like to accomplish, like improving your overall time or earning a medal at your next race.

But if you really want to set the most powerful goals possible, it's not enough to have a generalized idea of what you want – you need to know exactly what you want and how you are going to achieve it.

Now it's time to write down the goals you want to accomplish. Keep the following in mind:

1. Goals, by their nature, are meant to stretch your capabilities. You need to find the balance between a goal that gets you to the next level and the reality of how far you can go today. You can set a goal that will stretch you to your limits and end up being so ambitious that you abandon it. You can also set a goal so low that there is no challenge for you and you experience no real growth. Selecting appropriate and motivating goals is a key component to your overall success as an athlete.

2. Be specific. Include the what, how, where, when and who if it applies. Don't just write down that you want to improve your mile-time. Instead, decide how many seconds or minutes you want to shave from your time every month for the next 12 months. Is there is an event you'll compete in? Is there a team you'd like to beat? A trophy you want to win? Write it all down.

It's okay if you're not exactly sure what to write now. The point here is to put your goals on paper so that they become real and you can read them often. Throughout this week, we'll edit your goals until they're ready.

3. Prioritize your list. If goals are related stepping stones, be sure to list them in the order they need to be accomplished along with your timeframe. In many cases, it may be more appropriate to look at the timing of a goal rather than its importance.

Your goal list is a living document. Goals will change as your life changes. You could end up with an injury, a job change, start a family, or discover that your goal was too easy to achieve. Many things will influence your achievements; so don't become so rigid about your goals that they completely crumble in the face of change. Consider prioritization a fluid process with constant ebbs and flows.

If you want to ensure your goal's success, it's important to make sure that you've set goals that are meaningful and appropriate for your life right now.

Goals must have personal relevance, even if they are simply athletic on the surface. Gold medals and faster times can carry huge emotional and financial significance. For example, a gold medal could mean more opportunities for you and your family. A faster time could be an achievement that celebrates your parents' dedication to providing you with the best life possible. And all personal achievements impact your life and bring more confidence and growth - and higher goals. If your goal sparks a personal passion, drive and desire in you, it's more likely that you'll achieve it.

My Goals

Be as detailed as possible. Include dates, times, locations, who you need to include, etc. if applicable.

1. _____

_____

_____

_____

_____

2. _____

_____

_____

_____

_____

3. _____

_____

_____

_____

_____

4. _____

_____

_____

_____

_____

After your goals have been set, be sure to:

1. Create a detailed task list.

Each goal has a set of sub-goals, tasks and objectives. Break goals down into smaller, manageable steps. Decide what needs to be completed, and in what order.

2. Measure and track your progress.

It is important that you have a mechanism for measuring and tracking your goals as you work through them. Measurement can mean many things. It can refer to the time it takes to get something done or the amount something changes. Determine your metrics and stay on track.

3. Use your support system.

If you want to be successful, you can't always do it alone. Understanding your strengths and weaknesses is important. When you need help, look to others for support. Your family members, friends, and training partner can provide a great background for support, especially if you're putting in long hours in training and need the emotional and mental benefits that come from healthy interpersonal relationships.

4. Embrace challenges and roadblocks.

Things never quite go as planned, no matter how hard you try. When those challenges come up - and they will - you need to be resilient. Do not let them derail you. Have a solid plan in place to deal with any setbacks or unforeseen events that may come your way.

5. Re-group and revise.

A planned route sometimes changes. What was a straight path may suddenly have a curve. If you don't follow the new path, you could very well end up in a ditch. Don't be afraid to reevaluate and adjust your goals if circumstances change or if you decide that you need to reprioritize what you want to accomplish.

6. Use self-discipline and remain focused.

It is so easy to let the day-to-day demands of living get in the way. Make it a daily task to review your goals and progress. Schedule your workouts and goal reviews and do them. Use your highlight reel to keep yourself motivated.

7. Raise the bar as you improve.

You don't want to become complacent or stagnant, so make sure you stretch yourself each time you reach a goal. Set your new goal just a bit higher and challenge yourself. Review Week 4 if you need to.

Now that you have your goals set, let's learn how to build your mental toughness. It will serve you well when the going gets rough.

Week Five: Building Your Mental Toughness

We've all heard about a "winning mindset." People with winning mindsets are more likely to take risks and be actively involved in the things that matter to them. They're more likely to be happy, healthy, and productive. They are super achievers on their way to the top!

But when it gets down to it, what exactly is a "winning mindset?" Is it a one-size-fits-all concept, where you have to "fake it until you make it?"

Or, does a winning mindset require a separate kind of approach, where each of us has our own certain attitude that propels us closer to the successes that make athletic accomplishments that much more meaningful?

It isn't about blocking out the world entirely; instead, it's about creating the kind of mindset that minimizes negative chatter and enhances positivity in your life. It's the kind of mindset that knows no matter how many times you fall down, you're always capable of picking yourself back up. In short, it's the mindset of a winning athlete.

Winning in and of itself is a finite concept with infinite connotations. In other words, winning can mean earning a blue ribbon at a horse show, placing first in the 400 meter dash or even just getting up in the morning when your body is screaming for you to stay in bed and pull the covers over your head.

Winning means pushing yourself to be your very best. A winning mindset blends together the traditional definition of "winning" (being your best) with your own personal spin on things (being your best at the things that matter most to you). For example, a winning mindset for an Olympic athlete means having the attitude that allows her to train for hours each day and eat a beneficial diet. On the other hand, a winning mindset for a cancer patient means having the strength to live his life each day and continue doing the things he loves without letting the illness take over his life.

In that respect, there is no such thing as a one-size-fits-all winning mindset. The sooner you embrace this realization, the sooner you can find the winning mindset that will unlock your true potential.

I've found that people who have optimized their winning mindset are those who can see the "bigger picture." Without a larger, more objective perspective, we're more susceptible to the daily influences and judgments that try to label us and stuff us in a limiting box. When we define ourselves by how many medals we've earned or how we stack up to someone else, we begin to lose sight of the truly wonderful potential each and every one of us has. Seeing the bigger picture, we realize that personal dramas don't matter. We accept that we will make mistakes – and when we do, it's not an indictment on who are as a person. It's just a result of taking a chance and it not working out as we'd planned.

On that note, I want to point out what should always be the first step towards achieving your own winning mindset – accepting the fact that you <u>will</u> make bad decisions, mistakes and missteps.

In that light, it becomes obvious that we should expect to earn a few bumps and bruises on the path we call life – and when we do, it's not in our best interest to punish ourselves for it. Instead, we can pick ourselves up, dust ourselves off and explore the WHY's of the mistake. Then we create a plan to do it better next time.

To achieve a winning mindset, it's important to let go of your past, no matter how much you think it played a role in forming the person you are today. Don't put a good or bad label on any of your past behaviors or experiences. Instead, simply derive meaning from it.

For example, if you lost a big race or came from a background where you didn't have access to the best training possible, don't let these experiences teach you to abuse or fear the love of others. Derive meaning from the experience. Show yourself how much stronger you are because of the experience. Write down the life lessons you've learned that have helped you become a better person. Even if you don't believe in the lessons you're writing down, do it anyway. Sometimes it takes seeing it on paper to realize just how much we can be influenced by our past, and how past experiences can keep us emotionally and mentally paralyzed if we let them.

Adopting a winning mindset also involves identifying and accepting the things in life that are beyond your control. I like to call these things "the facts of life." Sometimes they deal with toxic scenarios and situations that are designed to drag you down or distract you from being the best you can be. For example, if you find that you're constantly comparing yourself to other athletes, you haven't yet accepted the facts of life. There will always be someone who is bigger or faster than you. Accepting this means that you'll be able to focus your energy on creating your winning mindset and applying it to every facet of your life from training and diet to personal health and fitness.

A Few "Facts Of Life"

Read these over and over until you've memorized them – the sooner you can accept the facts of life, the sooner you can let go of the doubt and lack of confidence that is keeping you from being your absolute best:

* Own your feelings, emotions, experiences and problems. Don't blame others.

* Don't expect others to rescue you. You are responsible for yourself.

* You are not entitled to anything.

* Your mind, body and spirit don't simply deteriorate with age. Lack of exercise in any of these areas causes deterioration.

* No one "completes" you. You are complete.

* You make the decision to be a contender or a pretender.

* Discipline will always be a key factor that determines your destiny.

* If you don't take action often, you'll eventually stop moving all together.

* Every day, you either get a little better or a little worse.

* You are the result of the choices you make.

* The best way to stand out is to be your best self.

Sometimes we doubt our ability to believe in our power and strength to move to the next level. But build your winning mindset and you'll believe in your own strength to win, no matter how lofty your goal or how big the obstacle in front of you might be.

In Week 6, you'll discover how to emulate the world's greatest athletes.

Week Six: How to Emulate Great Athletes

Congratulations – You've reached Week Six!

You've got your support system in place, created your highlight reel, set some powerful goals, started work on developing your mental toughness, and more. You are well on your way to becoming the A+ athlete you were always meant to be.

Week Six is a fun one. We're going to talk about the importance of emulating great athletes, no matter what sport they play. Notice that I said <u>emulate</u>, not worship. There's a big difference between hero worship – where your role model can do no wrong, even when he or she has displayed awful behaviors – and emulation, where you use your athlete as a platform for learning important lessons and behaviors that can be applied in your own life.

There's another distinct difference between hero worship and emulation. With the former, you're likely to view the athlete's accomplishments as your own. In other words, if he or she wins a match, you'll feel like you won as well. Suddenly, you're holding that athlete's performance as more important than your own – and that can have a significant impact on your game.

Emulation, on the other hand, teaches you to derive important meaning from your favorite athlete's experiences so you can apply it to your own life. If your favorite athlete gets embroiled in a personal scandal, you'll learn that it's always important to be a good person, whether you're on or off the field. Should your athletic hero's performance suddenly take a dive, you can use this as a lesson about the importance of continued improvement (or at the very least, how to retire gracefully).

Exercise 6.1

Create a list of your favorite athletes. Don't limit your list to people who play your sport or are currently active. If you love Michael Jordan, or you admire Gertrude Ederle, the first woman to swim across the English Channel in 1928, go ahead and add them to the list. You may include local athletes too, even whole teams. Be sure to include the reasons why they inspire you.

1. _____

Why?_____

_____

2. _____

Why?_____

_____

3. _____

Why?_____

_____

4. _____

Why?_____

_____

5. _____

Why?_____

_____

Note: if you can't come up with any compelling reasons why someone is on your list, choose someone else.

Here are a few more strategies you can use to successfully emulate – not worship – your favorite athlete:

- Use the athlete to set the bar high in your own life. Instead of seeing your favorite athlete as someone who is completely untouchable – and therefore, intimidating – see him or her as an example to follow. Study up on the athlete's diet, discipline, and practice regimen. While you don't have to copy them exactly (especially if they're professional and you're just starting out in the sport), they can give you a good idea of the hard work and dedication it takes to get to that level.

- Look for other athletes who are similar to your role model. Ideally, you want to find as many athletes as possible to emulate, as there are different lessons you can learn from each individual. You don't have to find athletes who encompass every lesson you'd like to learn; instead, find athletes who display characteristics you'd like to emulate in your own life. For example, maybe there's one athlete whose dedication you admire, while another may have a great sense of team spirit. There's no rule that says you have to stick to just one role model, so feel free to expand your horizons.

- Think about what it is about that athlete that resonates with you. When you first heard of that athlete, what immediately stuck out to you? What did you admire the most? Getting in touch with the reasons why that athlete speaks to you can help you identify the qualities and characteristics you'd like to display in your own life.

- Don't limit your search for a role model to the professional or even collegiate level – an ideal athlete can be someone who trains in your gym, or even your coach or personal trainer. There's inspiration everywhere, so don't limit yourself to just one type of athlete.

- If you get the chance to connect with the athlete you want to emulate, don't be afraid to ask for advice or guidance about how you can improve your own performance. Athletes are often more than happy to help others, so don't feel as if you're crossing a line. Of course, you should be mentally prepared to be let down by your role model. For example, if you get the chance to approach a professional athlete and they brush you off, don't take it personally. They're human beings after all, and they might not have the time or the energy to give everyone the personal attention that they want.

Remember, there are important lessons to be learned when you emulate your athletic role model. Study how that athlete successfully approaches various challenges in his or her life, and seek to embrace those winning types of behaviors in your own life. Tweak his or her behaviors to match your own life and personality type. After all, you're not seeking to become an identical clone of your favorite athlete; you're simply trying to learn important lessons and see what works for you.

Now that you've reached the end of the *Mind Over Head Chatter* course, you're ready to start to use your head chatter to your advantage.

To build your support network...

Set more powerful goals...

Achieve peak performance levels...

And unlock the kind of benefits that are only possible when your mind truly believes in your ability to become a success.

So now that you've finished the *Mind Over Head Chatter* six-week course, there's only one question I have for you:

Are you ready to bring your A-game?

Mind Over Head Chatter Goal Worksheet

NAME: _____ DATE: _____

MY GOALS:

1. _____

2. _____

3. _____

4. _____

5. _____

My #1 goal now is #_____

I AM GIVING MYSELF _____ MONTHS TO ACHIEVE THIS GOAL.

I COMMIT TO DOING THE FOLLOWING TO ACHIEVE THIS GOAL:

_____

_____

_____

I WILL USE THE FOLLOWING TRAINING PLAN:

_____

_____

_____

_____

I WILL DESIGNATE_____AS MY WEEKLY DAY TO TRACK MY PROGRESS.

Bonus Material

Creating a World Class Mindset
By Greg Justice, MA

Presented at the 2015 Mindset Performance Institute Summit
Greenwich, CT - July 25, 2015

When I give a presentation, I always like to introduce at least two individuals who have impacted my business and life.

Fred Hatfield, Ph.D. (aka Dr. Squat) currently serves as the President of the International Sports Sciences Association (ISSA). He is a best-selling author, speaker and three-time World Champion powerlifter. Dr. Hatfield's most memorable accomplishment in sport came at age 45 when, at a body weight of 255 lbs, he lifted 1014 lbs. in the squat (1987), more weight than any man in history had ever lifted successfully in competition. He was inducted into the Powerlifting Hall of Fame in June of 2000.

Henry Bloch is the co-founder and honorary chairman of the board of **H&R Block**, which he and his brother, Richard, founded in 1955. Mr. Bloch resides in the Kansas City area and is widely known as a businessman, civic leader and supporter of the arts and education who works to improve the quality of life in his hometown of Kansas City.

What Does It Take To Create a World Class Mindset?

There are three main ingredients:

- Motivation
- Visualization
- Belief (You Gotta Believe)

I. Motivation

Some say that love makes the world go 'round but, *passion* is the fuel for positive emotions and higher performance levels in any endeavor. Research shows that it's passion which inspires us all with psychological well-being, life satisfaction and a solid, growing sense of self...it's the fire deep down in the belly of a Champion!

Professional motivators go to extremes to "fire up" participants, to inspire them and trigger a charge of enthusiasm. But ask any professional athletics advisor, and he or she will tell you that the true fire gets ignited by a dream and that dream is fueled by passion. It comes from within, not from the outside, or by listening to another person.

Passion, according to the dictionary, is defined as a strong inclination to an activity that is self-defining, that a person loves, finds important, and in which regular time and energy are invested.

Over the past decade, the field of psychology has taken an interest in passion. A number of studies have been conducted on the subject and have subsequently led to the publication of professional papers that describe two types of passion--harmonious and obsessive.

Harmonious passion springs from an autonomous internalization of a specific activity into one's identity. Research shows that harmonious passions contribute to continuous and ever expanding psychological well-being. Harmonious passions help prevent negative experiences, like psychological conflicts and the sense of being ill at ease.

Obsessive passion, on the other hand, springs from a controlled internalization rather than an autonomous one, and it eventually comes to control a person, rather than to inspire or enhance one's life.

Research also indicated that with obsessive passion, less that optimal - and even negative - outcomes may be experienced.

Here's what Dr. Hatfield had to say about passion:

"Passion is not your need to achieve.
Instead, it's a burning desire to exceed all bounds.

It is not commitment to excellence.
It's utter distain for anything less.

It's not endless hours of practice.
It's perfect practice.

It's not your ability to cope.
It's the total domination of every situation in life.

It's not setting unrealistic goals or vague goals.
Because goals all too often prescribe performance limits.

It's not doing what it takes to win.
It's doing what it takes to exceed the bounds of mere convention.

Most of all, it's not the force of skill or muscle.
Rather, it's the explosive, often calamitous, force of will.

Now, if you believe in and practice these things, then for you, winning is neither everything, nor the only thing…for you, winning is a foregone conclusion."

You can see and listen to my entire interview with Fred Hatfield at:

https://aycfit.wistia.com/medias/17cl6bo719

II. Visualization

There's an anonymous quote that goes, "It's not who you are that holds you back, it's who you think you're not."

There are overwhelming psychological and performance benefits that occur when you cast yourself as the star of your own highlight reel. I'm not talking about a literal version of actual events, but rather a developing "film" your imagination creates of yourself performing or achieving your goals.

Now is the opportune time to be the writer, director, producer and actor in the personal highlight reel of your mind.

Highlight reels are typically thought of as those special moments on the sports news screen, but highlight reels don't always have to be factual taped events. The best viewing can occur right in your own head. And, to make it even better, that highlight reel does not have to be based on facts as they are now, but rather on your vision for the future.

Personal highlight reels aren't like a static photo finish. They're a dynamic embellishment of the individual's wishes, dreams, and hopes all layered onto an experience or all-encompassing concept. Don't fall into a trap of feeling lessened by learning about someone else's highlight reel. Avoid comparing someone else's reel to what you know yours to be from your own personal place of behind-the-scenes reflection. Chances are you could very well be comparing your weakest moment to someone else's strongest. Keep your own highlight reel playing, and keep it in focus.

If you've never tried visualizing before, here are some tips on how to do it:

* Your inner eye is your camera as you imagine your scene.

* Pay attention to your senses: sight, hearing, smell, taste, and touch, to experience all the details.

* Be aware of the results you wish for.

* Note how you feel when you are doing your best, when you have done your best, and when you see yourself successful and winning.

* If something goes wrong, replay your scene and fix it.

* You can watch your visualization at whatever speeds you wish--slowing down or speeding up.

* Allow yourself to experience elated emotions and give yourself credit for your successes, for your job well done.

* Repeat your visualization many times so your head and body will be trained to be stronger each time.

* With practice, you can authentically experience what you are imagining, even with sounds and smells, as long as you get into the realistic "nitty-gritty" of the whole--how you felt.

- Why is visualization so important? Because, the human mind cannot distinguish between a real and visualized experience.

III. Belief (You Gotta Believe)

How do you spell success? There are actually three C's that you'll need to remember in order to achieve success: **Confidence**, **Courage** and **Commitment**.

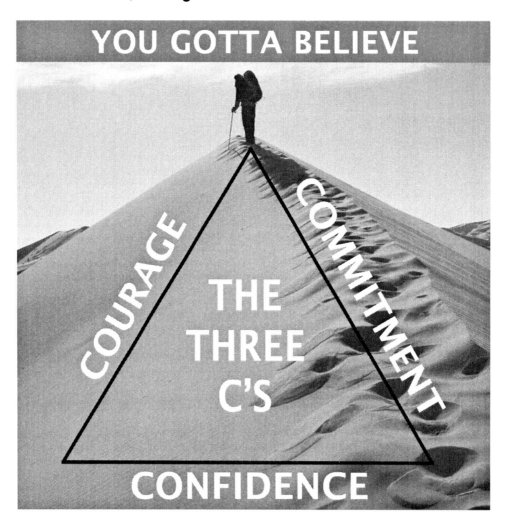

I like to use the visual of a triangle with "confidence" at its base. Courage and commitment are built on confidence.

Confidence is the quality that motivates you to accept and accomplish what might otherwise seem too difficult or impossible. Confidence keeps you working hard even though there may be setbacks along the way.

Confidence is like a cousin to positive mental thinking. It's what gives you the courage to focus on strengths in the face of challenges.

The sky's the limit, as the saying goes.

I recently had a conversation with one of my long time clients, Henry Bloch (H of H&R Block) about confidence. Below is the document I created that includes Henry's advice.

7 Steps to Build & Maintain Confidence
(Created as Part of a Conversation w/ Henry Bloch)

1. …And then some.

    Whether it's in your business or personal relationships, or any endeavor, you should always do what's expected of you…and then some.

2. Stay focused on yourself and what you control.

    Don't compare yourself to others, just focus on how you can do your very best and everything else will take care of itself.

3. Reward your daily victories.

    Don't disregard the small victories. Write them down, as they serve as confidence builders.

4. Forgive yourself for setbacks or mistakes.

    Don't dwell on mistakes, but forgive yourself and move forward.

5. Keep a feedback journal.

    Record your thoughts right after a big meeting or performance, to see if you can identify any lapses in confidence.

6. Know your own self confidence builders.

    What works best for some may not work for others, so know what works for you. Perhaps it's a pep talk, or surrounding yourself with supportive people who believe in you.

7. Use powerful affirmations, as part of your self-talk.

    Use "I am, I will, I have" rather than "I want, or I hope".

The next C, **Courage,** consists of bravery, perseverance, integrity and honesty. Studies on fear and courage have identified five factors as part of courage.

The first factor is determination. The word determination comes from Latin, meaning limiting. Determination is a part of personality that would push on despite limits or barriers. Examples would be "I perform to my best ability no matter the conditions, even under pressure," or, "I always have my goals in sight."

The second factor is confidence/mastery. Confidence is the belief an athlete has that he or she can perform a desired behavior successfully. Mastery is related to the performance of a skill and to the level of accomplishment. Confidence is a major part of mastery.

The third factor is assertiveness - using acceptable physical force with no intent to injure, with an unusually high degree of effort to achieve a goal. An example would be "I like to take the initiative when faced with difficulties, I assert myself even when facing dangerous situations.

The fourth factor is venturesome/coping with fear and risk taking. In high-level sports, risk taking behavior should be present. One researcher described sports as a culture of risks with acceptance of playing through the possibility of pain or injury, and coping with fear in the face of high risk or danger. Exercise in itself is a type of health risk management. An athlete might say, "I risk injury so that I won't lose." or, "I perform my best even in the face of injury."

The fifth factor is sacrifice behaviors/altruism. In sports, you might hear a player say, "I do not hesitate to compete even when faced with possible defeat," or, "I defend my beliefs even if this action could be harmful to me."

The third C, **Commitment,** could be described as "the heart of human excellence, the overall perspective, the way one views the self, and the capacity for importance of the pursuit and desire to become the best."

There are five supporting elements to commitment. They are: full focus, positive images, mental readiness, distraction control, and constructive evaluation.

Commitment is an essential ingredient in the pursuit of excellence. It is about committing the self to be the best you can be and continually working to make improvement to persist through ups and downs. It's a commitment to the goal of excelling which ignites and drives you daily to act in ways that lead to excelling. This means committing to high quality mental, physical and technical preparation, clear goals, and relentless pursuit of them.

If you're unsure about your level of commitment, ask yourself these questions:

Are your goals clear, challenging and targeted at being your best?

Do you work at improving something each day?

Will your commitment to training be enough to take you to your high level goals?

Is your commitment to respecting your personal needs for balance, strong enough to reach your goals?

Traditionally there has been too much emphasis put on confidence alone as the primary characteristic of success. However, confidence without both commitment and courage is like a high-performance Indy car without any fuel in the gas tank--it may look like a winner, but can't get very far.

Seeing success as the triangle formed from the three Cs, along with confidence as the base and commitment and courage as the supporting sides, helps you stay "pointed" in the right direction.

The qualities that make a World Class Mindset are not reserved for the lucky or chosen. All the qualities that I have covered reveal that a World Class Mindset is composed of attributes anyone can develop.